Schnauzers as Pets

The Ultimate Guide for Schnauzers

Schnauzers General Info, Purchasing, Care, Cost, Keeping, Health, Supplies, Food, Breeding and More Included!

By Lolly Brown

Copyrights and Trademarks

All rights reserved. No part of this book may be reproduced or transformed in any form or by any means, graphic, electronic, or mechanical, including photocopying, recording, taping, or by any information storage retrieval system, without the written permission of the author.

This publication is Copyright ©2017 NRB Publishing, an imprint. Nevada. All products, graphics, publications, software and services mentioned and recommended in this publication are protected by trademarks. In such instance, all trademarks & copyright belong to the respective owners. For information consult www.NRBpublishing.com

Disclaimer and Legal Notice

This product is not legal, medical, or accounting advice and should not be interpreted in that manner. You need to do your own due-diligence to determine if the content of this product is right for you. While every attempt has been made to verify the information shared in this publication, neither the author, neither publisher, nor the affiliates assume any responsibility for errors, omissions or contrary interpretation of the subject matter herein. Any perceived slights to any specific person(s) or organization(s) are purely unintentional.

We have no control over the nature, content and availability of the web sites listed in this book. The inclusion of any web site links does not necessarily imply a recommendation or endorse the views expressed within them. We take no responsibility for, and will not be liable for, the websites being temporarily unavailable or being removed from the internet.

The accuracy and completeness of information provided herein and opinions stated herein are not guaranteed or warranted to produce any particular results, and the advice and strategies, contained herein may not be suitable for every individual. Neither the author nor the publisher shall be liable for any loss incurred as a consequence of the use and application, directly or indirectly, of any information presented in this work. This publication is designed to provide information in regard to the subject matter covered.

Neither the author nor the publisher assume any responsibility for any errors or omissions, nor do they represent or warrant that the ideas, information, actions, plans, suggestions contained in this book is in all cases accurate. It is the reader's responsibility to find advice before putting anything written in this book into practice. The information in this book is not intended to serve as legal, medical, or accounting advice.

Foreword

Schnauzers make great pets for anyone who leads an active lifestyle. They are active, agile, intelligent, and highly robust and are reliable companions. They have great endurance and are strong canines. The standard schnauzer is also highly independent and is classified as possessing ideal traits of the working dog group.

Standard Schnauzer's are lively animals whether indoors or out, showing impressive agility and athletic prowess. They love to play and they need regular exercise (just as we do!) and also needs a lot of space to run in order to spend that seemingly indispensable energy.

Now if you think you are ready for and want a canine companion who is sturdy, with a good size physique or one who is graceful, athletic, agile, and elegant all at once, light on their feet and sensitive of your moods, a standard Schnauzer could be the perfect canine to bring home.

Table of Contents

Chapter One: Biological Information 1

    History of Schnauzer Dogs 2

    Taxonomy and Origin 4

    Size, Life Span, and Physical Appearance 6

    Fun Trivias 7

Chapter Two: Schnauzers as Pets 9

    Is the Standard Schnauzer the Right Pet for You? 10

    Temperament and Behavioral Characteristics 16

    Behavioral Characteristics with other Pets 17

    Pros and Cons of Standard Schnauzers 19

    Travel License for Dogs 19

    Cost of Owning a Dog 20

Chapter Three: Purchasing and Selecting a Healthy Standard Schnauzer Breed 31

    How to Purchase a Standard Schnauzers Breed from Reputable Breeders 34

    Good Breeder vs. Bad Breeder 35

Chapter Four: Habitat Requirements 41

    Housing Temperature 45

Chapter Five: Nutrition and Feeding 53

    Nutritional Needs of Standard Schnauzer 54

    Types of Commercial Dog Foods 59

    Toxic Foods to Avoid 63

    Tips in Feeding Your Standard Schnauzer 66

Chapter Six: Grooming and Training Your Standard Schnauzer 67

    Training and Dealing with Your Dog's Behavior 69

    Training Tips for Your Standard Schnauzers 70

    Housebreaking Tips for your Standard Schnauzers 71

Chapter Seven: Showing Your Schnauzers 73

Chapter Eight: Breeding Your Schnauzer 83

    Breeding Basics 84

    Raising Puppies 86

Chapter Nine: Common Illnesses of Schnauzer Dogs 89

    Vaccinations for Puppies and Adult Dogs 92

    Vaccination Schedule 93

    First Aid Treatments 93

Conclusion 95

Photo Credits 97

References 99

Chapter One: Biological Information

The standard schnauzer was once bred to catch rats, pests and were known to be (and still are) great guard dogs. The giant schnauzer as well as the miniature one were bred out of the standard schnauzer and were the outcome of outcrosses with other breeds which exhibited favorable traits requires for the original purpose of the moustache canine.

These be-moustache canines which show absolute loyalty and display great friendliness are energetic and protective animals who show love and tenderness coupled with every trait a dog owner would want in a companion canine. They are alert and will signal housemates of possible dangers or threats. However, its innate persistence could often lead to relentless barking. This trait can be curbed by a potential owner by getting the canine into proper training. The standard schnauzer is highly independent and is classified as possessing ideal traits of the working dog group.

History of Schnauzer Dogs

It was in the 1800's when German breeders took an interest in standardizing the Schnauzer breed. During that period, cross breeding with black German Poodles and gray Wolfspitz produced the distinct color and texture of the schnauzer. It was also during this period when the Standard Schnauzer was cross bred with other breeds to come up with the Miniature Schnauzer and after which followed the Giant Schnauzer.

During those early years up until the late 1800s, Standard Schnauzers were known as Wirehaired Pinschers. It was in 1879 when they were first shown at the German International Show in Hanover. It was a canine named Schnauzer who placed first and brought home the prize that year. Since the 1880s, a breed standard was written up with

Chapter One: Biological Information

the first specialty show held in 1890 at Stuttgart. Ninety three dogs were listed as entry candidates that year.

When the 1900s rolled in, the breed became more and more popularly known as the Schnauzer. This was possibly due to the fact that the standard schnauzer sported a be-moustache look and probably largely due to this first canine-sort winner whose name was "Schnauzer".

It has been documented that several Standard Schnauzers were brought into US shores during the early 1900s. The distinctly unmistakable Schnauzer was so dearly loved by their humans that they were brought over by immigrants from Germany and American travellers who saw and fell in love with these adorable canines. It wasn't until after WWI when the breed was imported.

It was in 1925 when the first Schnauzer Club of America was formed. The club later on split in 1933 and formed two separate organizations, namely, the American Miniature Schnauzer Club and the Standard Schnauzer Club of America.

Chapter One: Biological Information

Taxonomy and Origin

Another magnificent dog which originated from Germany during the 15th and 16th century, the Schnauzer got its name from the German term for snout and is the colloquial word for "moustache", mainly because of its appearance of having one. The schnauzer does not have the typical terrier temperament but are considered a terrier-sort of canine.

They are highly intelligent canines with super high energy levels therefore getting them into training early is a strong recommendation if you want to keep the peace with your neighbors. Since they are highly energetic canines, it is also recommended that they have daily exercise to spend their energy positively. There are, presently three different sorts of schnauzers; the miniature, the standard and the giant schnauzer.

The miniature schnauzer makes for excellent companions because they are not the aggressive sort. However they will sound the alarm when they think there is a threat. The miniature schnauzer resulted from the crossbreeding of the original schnauzer with other breeds like the affenpinscher and the poodle. The miniature is a

Chapter One: Biological Information

delicate sort and is recommended to be kept as an indoor pet.

The standard schnauzer, and the focus of our book, is around 1.5 feet tall from the shoulders and weighs in at around 30 to 45 pounds, or about 14 to 20 kilograms. The German Standard Schnauzer, and the limelight of this book, is classified under the working dog group. They have been employed to be rat and pest catchers by breeders of the past. The standard schnauzer, being the working dog that it is, was also employed to carry messages during the war. It aided the Red Cross and has also been utilized as police dogs.

The giant schnauzer measures in at about two feet or about 61 cm from the shoulder and weighs in between 55 to 80 pounds or about 25 to 36 kg. The giant schnauzer is also classified as a working dog and came about from breeding in Swabia during the 17th century. It is a variant of the pinscher breed and has a rough coat of fur. The giant schnauzer was independently bred through cross breeding with Great Danes, German Shepherds, Rottweilers, Boxers, Bouvier des Flandres, Muncheners, Dobermans, Thuringian Shepherds, and the Standard Schnauzer. The Giant Schnauzer was bred for the purposes of guarding farms and driving livestock to market.

Chapter One: Biological Information

In the United States, the Schnauzer was classified as a terrier and this is how the Miniature Schnauzer is organized up to this day. However, since the Germans always classified the Standard Schnauzer as a working dog, the AKC reclassified and put it in the Working Group classification in 1945. It presently ranks 99th amongst the varieties of recognized breeds by the AKC.

Size, Life Span, and Physical Appearance

The standard male schnauzer is about 18 20 inches tall from its shoulders and would weigh anywhere from 35 and 58 pounds or around 16 to 26 kilograms. The standard female schnauzer weighs in at about 30 to 45 pounds or 14 to 20 kg and is about 17 to 19 inches high or 43 to 48 cm.

Schnauzers are often bred multi - colored or white and sometimes they come with brown fur. However, these colors are not accepted by the American Kennel Club. The coat colors of schnauzers approved by the American Kennel Club are black, black and silver as well as salt and pepper.

Schnauzers look quite distinct with their long fluffy, scruffy eyebrows and very distinct bearded faces. The standard schnauzer has wiry, harsh coating when hand-

Chapter One: Biological Information

stripped. Their fur is soft and supple when clipped or trimmed with scissors.

The Standard Schnauzer has an average lifespan of about 13 to 16 years and some have reportedly lived longer lives with proper care.

Fun Trivias

- Teacup and toy schnauzers are not actually schnauzers but are commonly termed this way for marketing purposes. The standard schnauzer has been popular subjects for painters like Sir Joshua Reynolds, Rembrandt and Albrecht Durer, however, proof of these paintings have yet to be seen.
- The standard schnauzer was a subject of a tapestry made by Lucas Cranach the Elder 1501.
- A statue of a hunter stands erect in the German marketplace of Mecklenburg which dates back to the 14th century and the hunter statue includes a canine, closely conforming to the present-day show Standard of a Schnauzer which crouches at the feet of the hunter statue.
- Canines are said to have magnificent olfactory sense and are great detectors of human emotions as well as, sometimes, illnesses. One Standard Schnauzer named

Chapter One: Biological Information

George was greatly lauded to be able to detect cancer in a person.
- Standard Schnauzers have been used time and again in TV shows and have inspired many cartoon, manga and anime canine characters.

Chapter Two: Schnauzers as Pets

Standard Schnauzers make great pets for anyone who leads an active lifestyle. They are active, agile, intelligent, and highly robust and are reliable companions. They have great endurance and are strong canines. With the proper training given early on after you get your own schnauzer, you could live happily with your content buddy and be great neighbors with others.

Originally bred to be guard dogs, police assistant, farm dogs and beast herders, the standard schnauzer of today are versatile canines who are protective and loving of the family they come into just as effectively.

Chapter Two: Schnauzers as Pets

Is the Standard Schnauzer the Right Pet for You?

Compatibility of human and animal is very important when in consideration of a pet to bring home. Why it is vital is because human and pet need to be in tune with each other? Basically because you will both either have to keep up with each other or would have to mirror each other in terms of exuberance and love for action.

The breed you want to choose should be based on your personality type. If you are the kind of person who loves to explore new places, learn of new things, love the company of equally minded individual's then the Standard Schnauzer is indeed one who would match your personality type.

The Standard Schnauzer is a breed which is easily bored with repetition and needs to engage in varied activities which not only gets it to exercise but also stimulate its mind.

The Standard Schnauzer's nature is a combination of many things including a high-spirited temperament and absolute reliability. A person first notices the distinctly keen looks of the Schnauzer commenting on how some have a harder look to them than others. Some give off an air of being more serious, business-like and boldness. Others look a lot mellower and give off a sweeter aura about them.

Chapter Two: Schnauzers as Pets

Standard Schnauzer's are lively animals whether indoors or out, showing impressive agility and athletic prowess. They love to play and they need regular exercise (just as we do!) and need a lot of space to run about to spend that seemingly indispensable energy.

Stimulate your Standard Schnauzer not only physically but mentally as well, because this is just as important to their wellbeing and wellness. Being innately intelligent canines, they need mind stimulation and this can be carried out through obedience and agility training and will satisfy its mental needs. This doesn't only benefit your Schnauzer canine alone but it benefits the peace and order of the home too. A Standard Schnauzer left on its own will find its own recognizance and this will include the inspection of things and places you would not be too happy to deal with.

Most Standard Schnauzers will be aloof with and wary of strangers, however with correct socialization they are sensible beasts who are discriminating of who is a friend and who isn't. A lot of Standard Schnauzers are aggressive when other canines of the same gender are present.

Standard Schnauzers are considered to be amongst the smartest of all working dog breeds and usually possess good decision making skills making them really good problem solvers. They are a persistent and strong-willed bunch, hence, start training them young to enjoy a life of absolute joy with them.

Chapter Two: Schnauzers as Pets

Training them young is vital because if not, they may dominate over you and the household. You will need to let them know early on who the boss is or bear with a demanding dog who likes to be in control. If given the proper early training using upbeat methods, many owners will realize they can lead the dog and find Schnauzers to be highly trainable. They are highly sensitive of your moods and enjoy being in close proximity with you as they watch you.

Now if you think you are ready for and want a canine companion who is sturdy, with a good size physique, one who is graceful and athletic, agile and elegant all at once, light on their feet and sensitive of your moods, a Standard Schnauzer could be the perfect canine to bring home.

If you want a dog that will mirror your active lifestyle and thrives on athletic activities, one who is a keen watch and guard dog that is completely loyal and utterly protective of its human family, then the Schnauzer is definitely one to consider strongly. If you are considering a low maintenance, overall healthy companion who is confident, bold, and vigorous and one who can learn almost anything you teach it, then the Schnauzer just moved up higher on your consideration list.

On the other hand, if you have no tolerance for frequent exercising, for a canines excited, exuberant puppy-personality, occasional aggression with other animals (especially those smaller than them) then you should probably continue looking because as mentioned earlier the Schnauzer has a penchant to be a pretty strong-willed canine and would need a take-charge sort of an owner.

Still want a Schnauzer, you say? Well then you can avoid the hard work by choosing to adopt and adult Standard Schnauzer. Not only will you be doing a great solid on your end, but with an adult canine you will probably have the advantage of becoming friends with a trained canine. A lot of Standard Schnauzers have proven themselves to be free of the negative traits of an untrained pup. However, if you are still in consideration of raising one yourself, then going to a reputable breeder is your only other avenue of choice. With all the correct papers in place and with guarantees to back up its health you know that you couldn't possibly go wrong with this option.

Things you want to remember about the Standard Schnauzer:

- You will need to provide them with enough exercise and mental stimulation because Standard Schnauzers are an active breed.

- Standard Schnauzers want and require daily opportunities to spend their energy and to utilize their busy minds to do interesting stuff. Otherwise they become easily bored, and they will typically express this pent up frustration by barking and through destructive chewing.

- Give them enough opportunities for socialization. Almost all Standard Schnauzers possess protective instincts toward their human family when around strangers. They need a lot of exposure to friendly humans so they understand to recognize the normal traits of "good guys." This way they can identify the difference when someone acts abnormally. Without mindful socialization, they tend to be suspicious of everyone, which is challenging to live with.

- Animal aggression is inevitable behavior of the Standard Schnauzer. Therefore keep smaller, furry pets away from them and never leave them unsupervised even if they seem friendly to each other.

- Many Standard Schnauzers will display dominance or aggression toward other canines of the same gender. Others possess strong instincts to chase and seize felines and other fleeing creatures.

- They possess a strong temperament. Only the best of Standard Schnauzers would be versatile working dogs, and who would be capable of learning a great deal of things. However, keep in mind that they have an independent mind and usually would like to think for them and are not pushovers to train and rise. There are Standard Schnauzers who are willful and dominant and who would try to be the boss if allowed to get away with it. You will need to prove that you give the commands and the one who is the leader of the pack and be consistent with your actions, words and schedule

In other words, you have to teach your Standard Schnauzer to respect you. A canine who respects you will do what you instruct it to and will cease what they are doing when you tell them "No."

Keep this mind as well about the grooming needs of these fuzzy-faced canines. Standard Schnauzers need regular clipping of its nails and trimming of its coat every few months. Some breed purists would say that Schnauzer coats must never be clipped because clipping makes for a coat softer and therefore more prone to matting. What they advocate instead is hand-stripping - a process where each dead hair is yanked out so the new ones can grow in place of those pulled out.

The opinion of other Schnauzer owners is that stripping is too time-consuming and may be uncomfortable for the dog (however there are some dogs who seem not to mind the fur pulling, so learn to get to know your Standard

Schnauzer and which method of hair/coat shedding is best suited for the. There are also many groomers who won't do it anymore.

Temperament and Behavioral Characteristics

Standard schnauzers are awesome canines that are clever and easy going with people they are familiar with. They will not bark for unknown reasons but when they do detect any sort of threat or danger, they may react quite protectively of the people and territory they share with their humans.

They are a pretty stubborn sort because of their innate independence and it could take some time and a lot of patience to house trains them. So it is imperative to get them the proper training early on after you get them.

Standard schnauzers, being the intelligent canines they are, are easily bored with doing the same thing over and over. Exposing them to various activities will address this behavioral trait and get you moving as well. Your schnauzer is a great companion for runs, walks and just about anything else your active lifestyle calls for.

Schnauzers are self-assured canines and will sense weakness in their humans and if not curbed early, they could capitalize on this by lording it over the household. Be compatible with your buddy and let your Standard Schnauzer understand who the alpha of the home is.

This canine breed can be considered a fearless and curious one. Not the best combination when off its leash. So, if you are outside with your Standard Schnauzer, do not allow it to go off on its own without its harness. This is especially because of its natural instinct of catching anything small and furry.

Standard Schnauzer when properly bred, raised and trained is a reliable and a protective animal toward their human family and human children. Both children and Standards live to play and love doing so. Both are inquisitive and would investigate new and strange things, environment and surroundings. They love nothing more than to romp in the yard on a nice warm summer day or under crisp winter sunshine. Interaction between dogs and children must always be supervised by a responsible adult so as playtime never gets out of hand, or too rough.

Behavioral Characteristics with other Pets

Since one of their purposes before is to mainly catch rats, Schnauzers in general shouldn't be trusted with other small household pets including hamsters, gerbils, rabbits, and guinea pigs. Most Schnauzer breed seem to be okay with other kinds of cats, but proper introduction should be implemented.

The thing about Schnauzers is that they have been bred and have a natural instinct to chase after little furry animals and catch them. This could be an advantage or disadvantage for a family. Say you live in a farm where you tend to animals or grow crops and plants, then a Standard Schnauzer would be a great working dog and pet for you and your family. However, if you are a city dweller and live in, say, a neighborhood or apartment building where your neighbors have their own pets, it may spell disaster because Standard Schnauzers are pretty territorial. And if they have a smaller pet than your Schnauzer it may start chasing after the neighbors smaller pet. So be aware of your Schnauzers natural trait and keep it on a leash whenever you go out with it.

Should you have existing pets smaller than your Standard Schnauzer, you want to make sure that you separate them from each other at all times. It would matter very little if your Schnauzer grew up and was raised at the same time with the smaller pet, it would be heartbreaking if your Schnauzers instincts kicked in when you weren't looking. Again be sure that if you do have smaller pets that they are kept away from your Standard Schnauzer.

Chapter Two: Schnauzers as Pets

Pros and Cons of Standard Schnauzers

Standard Schnauzers are super loyal pets and would shower you and other people in the family with love and affection. This canine will be one of the most loyal friends you would ever know.

They are protective and will make good guard dogs for a family and not let you down in terms of providing added security toward danger or strangers. Standard Schnauzers are excellent search and rescue dogs and have been employed as such time and again.

They are excellent trackers and would be able to find anything that it is trained to discover and retrieve. They have been acclaimed to be one of the most perfect canines employed as therapy dogs. They are agile dogs and love exploring anything when given the opportunity.

Being excellent trackers can go either way depending on your purposes for taking in a Standard Schnauzer. They will go after anything furry, moving and smaller than them and will probably not relent until its instincts have been satisfied.

Travel License for Dogs

Your Schnauzer will need a passport to travel if you intend to bring it on overseas voyages, just like us humans.

Remember that you will also need a good sized crate to place your dog in for the duration of the flight. You may visit your local municipal hall to inquire about the steps you need to take when acquiring a passport for your canine. Keep in mind that you want to keep all medical records of the canine with you as well as any local licenses it may have during trips. When driving across state lines, authorities may ask for these papers and you will need to present them when asked.

Cost of Owning a Dog

Once out in the world, it would be just a matter of time until your Standard Schnauzer joins you and your family at home. It is crucial that you give it all that the Schnauzer would need and will require to feel at ease in their new home and feel welcome. Doing so will make for easier transition for you and canine to allow seamless integration into the family as well as the household.

Recognizing the financial implications of a new animal is a vital monetary detail you will want to work out very early on as you consider the inclusion of a Standard Schnauzer to your family. You will first need to find a breeder of upstanding repute to work with because as earlier mentioned; the history of the pup's parents will be crucial details which will give you an insight of the overall health of the Schnauzer pup.

The cost of schnauzer adult breed and puppies can cost anywhere between **$400** and **$1,500**. But if it is fine with you in getting pass the puppy stage or are looking to get a mature Standard Schnauzer instead, then breeds that is more than two years old can cost a lot lower price; usually around **$75** to **$400**. Generally speaking, female dog breeds will cost you more than males because of their birthing abilities.

Acquiring a healthy Standard Schnauzer will hinge on factors like its family history, availability of pups, quality of dog/s, and location from which it will be coming from, because if the canine is bought out of state or country there will be transportation costs and in some cases legalities which can't be avoided. The price of the Schnauzer will also greatly depend on whether the Schnauzer is a pet or show quality with the latter costing a lot more than the former.

Whatever the dollar price you shell out for your pet canine, remember that you must be given the Schnauzer's medical records. It has to have been given all its puppy vaccinations and should have been de-wormed with at least a minimum one year health guarantee.

Should the Schnauzer be coming from out of state or country, you would need to calculate and factor in shipping costs. The only way to determine this is to talk with people from shipping companies to find out handling fee details and final cost of shipping as well.

You will need to make a considerable investment in dog supplies such as grooming tools, food, an assortment of equipment, accessories, toys, and general sundries. These investments will not only solidify the presence of the Schnauzer within the home, these would also be crucial purchase investments which will help integrate the new addition Schnauzer to the family.

Here are some of the other important purchases you need to start building on before you take pick up and home your new Schnauzer buddy:

- **A dog crate** - a sturdy dog crate, if picked out correctly, will serve both you and your Schnauzer pet well for a long time. Put some money on a durable one because this will be one piece of equipment which will prove worthy of the bucks you spent over time. Transporting your Schnauzer canine to and from places will be a reality you will soon discover and you will certainly not want to put your pet in danger riding in any kind of vehicle without some form of protection. You will most certainly want to bring your Schnauzer dog with you for extended family trips or short term vacations so this will also conveniently double as its home away from home during these forays. A box crate also doubles as a good place to potty train your Schnauzer.

- **A bed** - the new family addition will require a place to rest its head just like you. Give your Schnauzer a sturdy bed, one which it can comfortably lounge in when it gets all tuckered out after an activity-filled day. Give your Schnauzer dog a special spot in the house to retreat to and get itself recharge when much needed rest is required.

- **A blanket** - a blanket equates to a world of familiar comfort to anyone. And this too is true for your Schnauzer buddy. Provide your Schnauzer dog a blanket which it can snuggle into when days and nights are cold. Its blanket can be placed on its bed or be put in a more social space of the home. It would also make a good alternative bed for quick, energizing naps.

- **Grooming brush** - A good brush down of the Schnauzers coat is going to be an essential routine you, or another adult in the family, will need to mind. The Schnauzer coat is thick and wiry and if not given the proper care your Schnauzer coat will have the tendency to tangle and mat. The amount of time you give your Schnauzer a thorough brushing will also be one good opportunity to inspect its skin, belly limbs, ears, eyes and other extremities. You want to keep in mind that the overall well-being of any pet, whatever breed it may be, shall be reflected in the animal's coat and skin. A coat, free of matting and tangling, is one sign of correct and proper nutrition. A skin free of bald patches, rashes, wounds and nicks is a skin to be envied. Make it a habit to brush your Schnauzer's coat to promote distribution of essential skin oils throughout its skin in order to stave off skin conditions or as a precaution, to detect the onset of any skin condition that might cause harm to your Schnauzer.

- **Toothbrush** - Your Schnauzer dog is going to need regular brushing to clean its teeth of food debris and plaque. Make sure you choose a toothbrush which will do the job right. You want to make certain that the brush fits the mouth of your Schnauzer comfortably and that it is sturdy enough to withstand any mischievous biting your Schnauzer is almost certain to give the brush. The prospective owner will also need to purchase pet approved toothpaste which will effectively clean the Schnauzer's teeth. Ask your local vet about the recommended cleaning toothpaste paste to use for your Schnauzer's teeth.

- **A nail trimmer or sander** - You need to routinely trim and/or sand your Schnauzer's nails and this task will come into the picture soon after the canine joins your family. You will probably have to experiment on tools which your Schnauzer will respond to with the least resistance. Some canines get antsy and very uncomfortable when their humans do the necessary work of clipping their nails, so it is crucial that you observe it and take mental notes about which tools and method of nail clipping your pet is agreeable to. If you use a cutter or a guillotine, be certain that you are cutting above the pink of the dog's nail. Accidentally cutting through the pink can cause heavy bleeding and utter discomfort to the dog which could lead to infection if left untreated. A sander might be gentler on the canine's senses, but the continuous whirring sound of the machine may cause discomfort to the Schnauzer's keen sense of hearing and a sander tends to heat up with prolonged use.

- **Stainless steel, slow-feeding bowls** - Slow-feeding bowls help in discouraging your canine from wolfing down food its food too fast and also from taking big gulps of water. Utilize these convenient slow-feeding bowls for its meals and drink during your Schnauzers feeding schedule. The bowl is made in such a way to promote slow-eating which allows your pet the luxury of enjoying each morsel of food you serve to it. A stainless steel feeding and drinking bowl will save you a ton of cash in the long run and provide you some peace of mind that the materials used to make the bowls are non-toxic and conveniently easy to clean.

- **A leash** - You will need to make use of a leash on your Standard Schnauzer dog as it undergoes canine training. A leash or harness will also come in handy and useful when you take it out for routine and much needed walks. Be sure to invest in a few which are sturdy, durable and ones which will last, especially for when your Schnauzer comes into maturity. A mature and full grown Schnauzer will be rambunctiously active therefore; a flimsy leash or harness may find you chasing after your Standard Schnauzer in the most inopportune of moments.

- **A fence** - a collapsible, folding fence can be used to create separation between other pets you have and a new addition. A folding fence can be utilized to give the pets a lot of much needed time to investigate and inspect each other; the fence will also serve as a safe barrier which will prevent them from getting any closer to each other before they are ready to share the same space. Keep in mind that small furry pets will have to be separated from the Schnauzer lest it mistake it for a rodent. A fence can also be used to hinder and prevent the canine from wandering out of an open door or into an uncovered pool.

- **Toys** - Your Standard Schnauzer will need toys and lots of it. Toys will be needed to engage the clever, intelligent and curious mind of your new Schnauzer dog buddy. Use toys to stimulate your canine's mind. This is a strong recommendation and one you should mind wisely and heed to if you want to avert the dog's boredom from creating an awful mess of a wreck in your home. The clever Schnauzer is one who requires to be engaged one way or another - physically and mentally - or it will channel all its energy on inanimate things around that house, like your furniture, which it will chew on, bite at, dig on, scratch into and shove around. Do not encourage or promote this destructive behavior, but instead select appropriate, toxic-free toys your Schnauzer can play with and ones which can be used by you and your pet during your own personal downtime with your new Schnauzer pet.

It is a given that you will discover other things your Standard Schnauzer will require to ensure a warm welcome

Chapter Two: Schnauzers as Pets

and a happy one at that, with you and your family. This is the perfect time to network with seasoned Standard Schnauzer dog owners and guardians to find out what worked and didn't work for them.

Keep in mind that solicited or unsolicited advice must be thought out and considered because no two canines have the exact same requirements. Ultimately it will be you and the immediate human family it comes in contact with daily who will know the needs and traits of the Schnauzer best, so, be alert, in tune with, aware and mindful of its needs.
Below is a short list of the primary and initial expenses you will need to consider which will give a potential Schnauzer owner an idea of the expenses and which will give you an overview of the expenses. This will help determine if you are financially ready to take in a Standard Schnauzer

Treats and Food -	$300 to $700
Canine Toys	$50 to $150
Harness and/or Leash	$25 to $75

Chapter Two: Schnauzers as Pets

Grooming (Supplies costs and/or Professional Grooming fees) -	$75 to $500
Veterinarian (From Shots, De-worming, Routine Medical Checkups, Health Issues) -	$200 to $1000
Medications (Heartworm, etc. and Supplements) -	$100 to $300
Annual Total:	$750 to $2725
Monthly Expense:	$62 to $227

Chapter Two: Schnauzers as Pets

Chapter Three: Purchasing and Selecting a Healthy Standard Schnauzer Breed

Standard Schnauzers are all-around canines whose original and primary purpose was to be guard and rat-catchers on German fields and farms. Their deep, throaty bark sounds as if it was coming from a much bigger dog, which makes them watchful and vigilant in carrying out their watchdog duties. Standard Schnauzers are highly resourceful hunters and effective retrievers in the water as well as on land.

Chapter Three: Purchasing and Selecting a Schnauzers

They are equally excellent sheep and cattle herders, as this is one of their primary jobs in a farm. Schnauzers are quick to sound off and bark at the any sign of trouble. They are protective by nature, are medium sized canines, resourceful, and loyalty to their human family which make them outstanding companions.

Before you consider talking to a breeder, and we encourage you to only deal with reputable ones, we want to encourage you to think about adoption. More mature dogs are typically housebroken, obedience trained and leads trained. Most of them are usually amiable to being groomed and brushed and even look forward to some quiet time after a robust runabout in the park.

Most adoptive Standard Schnauzers are males and over 5 years old. There are around 12- 15 Schnauzers placed for adoption through the Standard Schnauzer Rescue Program throughout the country. There are a number of reasons why the Schnauzers are given up for adoption, like, divorce, illness in human family, relocation to another country divorce, death and many other number of reasons. Adoption is another route you would want to think about. Should adopting a Standard Schnauzer be the route you choose to take, you will forever doubly feel the rewards and

Chapter Three: Purchasing and Selecting a Schnauzers

benefits of taking in a Standard Schnauzer which you would have ultimately saved from a bleak future.

Be mindful though that adopting a Standard Schnauzer, whether it be pup or full grown, mature dog, it will have its own set of challenges and issues which may differ a lot from what one would expect when purchasing a Standard Schnauzer from a breeder of good repute.

You will need to keep in mind that you might possibly be shelling out more cash if the dog comes from a home which neglected it, did not give it proper training, routine medical care, grooming attention and sufficient human interaction and socialization.

Prepared to be set back a little should the dog you adopt or rescue physical challenges or medical conditions. If this is the case, it is recommended that you ask as many questions about the canine's history. The information you get about the canine, no matter how little will somehow give you an idea of what may be later.

You may not get all the details of the Schnauzers history, which was previously discussed to be important, as you would have if the canine were bought from a reputable breeder. At this time your generous heart and willingness to take on the care of a possibly ill pet (as well as a deep well of resources) will be just what a rescue canine would need.

The good news is, once your new Schnauzer is welcomed to the eager arms of your household, your new

Chapter Three: Purchasing and Selecting a Schnauzers

pet Schnauzer will be given a new lease on life and a chance of a better future. This will cover you for good a good deed, well done. This would be an additional perk to the many more you will realize taking in a rescue Standard Schnauzer. The minute your new clever companion gets wind of what you had done for it, it will forever have your back and be your loyal companion, friend and guardian. Be ready to be showered with loving fondness and many years of good times.

How to Purchase a Standard Schnauzers Breed from Reputable Breeders

The health, wellbeing and future of all pedigreed pets depend primarily on two things. First is the history of the animal's parents. Second is the procedure used by breeders during the breeding and mating season with quality of food and nutrition trailing at a close second.

It is of great importance that, you, as a potential Schnauzer owner and guardian of this magnificent animal, find out and determine the methods used by breeders you will be dealing and doing business with. Keep away from pet shops and puppy mills at all costs and do not patronize these establishments. These kinds of businesses promote the growing instances of medical issues and ill health conditions

Chapter Three: Purchasing and Selecting a Schnauzers

detected in a lot of animals. Do not promote or take part in lining these establishments' pockets and from furthering their shady dealings, which is only set up for them to gain a quick buck. Avoid doing business with them.

In order to purchase and bring home a canine in the best of health, do not acquire an animal from an irresponsible breeder, a puppy mill or a pet shop. The problematic issues abound with irresponsible breeders and run aplenty. Should you decide to take your chances with this route then you will need to be aware that you are possibly setting yourself up for a mountain of medical fees, avoidable troubles and ultimately, heartache. The sufferings of a Standard Schnauzer pup that is passed down the medical conditions of its parents through shady breeding practices can be painful to live through and can most certainly be avoided.

Good Breeder vs. Bad Breeder

Unscrupulous breeders pay no attention or mind to how the breeding process is carried out as long as they get paid. They do not consider or take into account the outcome of the litter or the possible future illnesses and sufferings of the canine which is usually the result of their improper breeding methods. They are not inclined to follow standard breeding practices which will ensure the good health and

Chapter Three: Purchasing and Selecting a Schnauzers

future of a Schnauzer puppy. These breeders are only in business for one reason alone and that is to make a quick sale and big money. Stay as far away from and keep your distance from this sort of people and start looking elsewhere.

In order to sift out and recognize the upstanding breeders from shady, fly-by-night individuals, you will have to be mindfully observant of the facilities they have if you are allowed to come for a visit and you have to ask a lot of questions pertinent to the history of the animal. The breeders who are simply in it to gain money will express no regard for the future health, environment or well-being of the Schnauzer puppy. These people will not ask about the family the Schnauzer will eventually be joining or what you have done in order to prepare for its homecoming. They will not investigate if the future home the Schnauzer puppy is going to is a place which will welcome and take care of it at any and all cost - these breeders are only interested in you handing over the cash.

On the other hand, reputable and upstanding breeders are going to be concerned about the family and home the Schnauzer puppy will be joining and be part of, once it arrives. These breeders will ask you questions to find out if you are a serious and able guardian and future owner to this awesomely clever creature. Reputable breeders would

Chapter Three: Purchasing and Selecting a Schnauzers

have given the pup its initial vaccination and seen to the requirements of the Schnauzer puppy during the early days of the puppy's life even before the canines handed over to your care.

These upstanding breeders of prime repute will ask of the Schnauzer's ultimate place and role in your family as well as the area you will have to set up for it. These individuals will want to know and determine that the humans the puppy will be joining will be taking in the Schnauzer puppy with willingness and responsibility that the family or person understands the rewards and challenges of their sharing home with a Standard Schnauzer. Good breeders will want to determine that the young Schnauzer puppy will be joining humans who are ready to make the pup a part of the family and who will show it respect, courtesy, kindness, friendship and unconditional love. Good breeders will be curious to find out if you have gotten in touch with, talked to and consulted with a trusted and certified vet about the medical care and costs of keeping a Schnauzer healthy.

Ask around, network with seasoned Schnauzer owners and seek out reputable breeders who do medical screenings and tests breeding canines before deeming them fit and healthy to produce puppies. Make certain that it is understood and clear that the canines are free of passed down diseases which may be inherited by future puppy

Chapter Three: Purchasing and Selecting a Schnauzers

litters. It is crucial for you to ask and know the history of the sire and bitch in order to guarantee that no hereditary or congenital disease will plague the litter of pups later. Determine, as well, that the breeding duo is of good temperament and relatively calm.

Breeders of reputable standing and come highly recommended will have no qualms in allowing you to visit their facilities in order for the future Schnauzer owner to be part of the whole breeding process. These individuals shall be open to your inquiries and will gladly answer questions you may want to ask about the procedures they use when they select the mating pair. Responsible breeders would have set aside the Schnauzers records of milestones for when the buyer is unavailable to be there. Good and thoughtful breeders would be ready to give useful information in relation to the dam and sire as well as pass on to you utilitarian recommendations and tips on how to effectively care for your new Standard Schnauzer.

A reputable breeder should be able to present health certificates for both the Standard Schnauzer puppy's parents showing a bill of health clearing both stud and dame of hip dysplasia from the Orthopedic Foundation of Animals. The breeder should also be able to show proof of clearance for eye disease from both parents from the CERF.

Purchasing from a breeder who is a member of the SSCA will include a process of matching potential puppy

Chapter Three: Purchasing and Selecting a Schnauzers

buyer and pup, of building a partnership between buyer and breeder and to make sure of the well-being, and health of the puppy.

Aside from those potential Standard Schnauzer buyers will have to and should be provided with written contracts and agreements in relation to the deposit given for the pay, guarantees, possible replacement, terms of sale and if applicable, terms of ownership. One good source of information to find Standard Schnauzer puppies, should you be strongly inclined to acquire and take home one or two of them, would be with the American Kennel Club.

A reputable breeder should also hand over a Registration transfer or a signed AKC Registration Application. Breeders of good repute and good standing will hand over the Schnauzer puppy's complete medical records which would not only include a detailed instruction for the future health care of the Standard Schnauzer puppy but these papers would also include a complete record of its health.

At the time of purchase and transfer, the breeder, will also be handing over to the potential buyer a pedigree which shows AKC registered numbers and names of the grandparents and parents of the Schnauzer puppy.

Chapter Three: Purchasing and Selecting a Schnauzers

List of Breeders and Rescue Websites

These magnificent canines are not the easiest to find because they are not usually bred as frequently as other canine breeds. The optimal place to locate a Standard Schnauzer pup would be with a SSCA (Standard Schnauzer Club of America) member. These members are not just merely breeding Schnauzers for the money but they are dedicated individuals who aim to improve the continuity of the breed lineage.

Here are some websites to check out should you be strongly inclined to adding a Standard Schnauzer to your mix of the family:

<www.centarastandardschnauzers.com>

<www.blackhawkstandardschnauzers.com>

<CastlewoodStandardSchnauzers.com>

<www.myschnauzers.com>

<www.moxieschnauzers.com>

<www.wunderkindschnauzers.com>

<www.windsongstdschnauzers.com>

Chapter Four: Habitat Requirements

During this point of your research, you have come closer to getting to know more about the loyal and lovable Standard Schnauzer and what to expect when you decide to raise and live with one. It will be up to you and other adults in the family (or equally able caregivers) who will be sharing the responsibility of caring for and tending to the needs of the new Schnauzer. Responsibility of knowing what to provide your new canine companion is crucial. Get your home ready and outfitted to make room for your new pet and make sure that your new Standard Schnauzer comes home to a safe environment which you have mindfully dog-proofed.

Chapter Four: Habitat Requirements

This measure is not only for the dog's safety but also for the ultimate safety of each member of the family with whom it will share space and home.

Remember and keep in mind that bringing home a new pet is a responsibility which is not to be taken lightly. Pets will be largely dependent on you, and other equally responsible family individuals, for their everyday needs of attention, food, care, and affection. Knowing what to do in the event of unforeseen situations and /or medical emergencies will be on your shoulders. You will need to get to know your Standard Schnauzer and learn to recognize signs of illness, discomfort and/or changes in your canine's usual routines or habits because knowing so will help you determine if they are in need of medical attention.

The responsibility of being a Standard Schnauzer owner will require quite a bit from you and is a job not to be taken lightly. Indeed, your Schnauzer will thrive better as long as its owner and caregivers carry out their jobs toward the feisty, furry canine. With that being said, Standard Schnauzers will still need basic equipment and sundries to keep them healthy, happy, and occupied.

This section of this book is aimed to shed light on time tested recommendations that will ensure Schnauzers contentment whilst under your family's loving care.
Ideal Habitat for Your Dog

Chapter Four: Habitat Requirements

Your actively playful Standard Schnauzer will require its own area to move in and about most specially if it is left on its own for a good part of the day. Providing it a fenced off area where your Schnauzer can play, sleep and eat on its own will allow it get used to periodic solitude.

You want to store valuable decor and check that there are no breakable items within your new canines reach which it may tip over and break during the time you are away. Store away all favorite souvenirs, mementos, presents, expensive antiques and precious trinkets which may shatter in shards and injure the canine whilst you are away.

Almost all plants are toxic and dangerous to canines so make sure that you look up the chemistry of existing plants in and around your homestead. You will need to find out if these are safe for the new pet addition in your home. If you should discover the presence of toxic foliage in and around your home, don't take chances. Do make an effort to either replant them farther away from the area where your dog is allowed to be in or, better yet, switch them up with canine-friendly plants.

You will want to dog-proof and refit each room your Standard Schnauzer is allowed to go into. Fit sturdy child-proof locks and fasten cabinet doors where you keep your cleaning agents, bathroom supplies, as well as medicine - all of which can make your canine sick or worse. Hide and stash away any small items which if and when discovered

Chapter Four: Habitat Requirements

and played with by your Schnauzer, could be swallowed and get stuck in its throat or digestive tract.

Make certain that rubbish bins are snugly fitted with lids which will not come off in the event of it being tipped over. One other thing you will want to make a habit of is putting down the lids of toilets when not in use, just in case your Schnauzer wanders into the toilet and attempts to drink out of the toilet bowl. Tipping over and falling into an uncovered WC bowl is also a very dangerous situation your new Schnauzer puppy could go through which could cause it horrible distress per chance no one is at home to pay mind and give it immediate assistance.

In these recent days of advanced technology and our seemingly never ending want of gadget upgrades, electric wires run aplenty and snake around our living spaces. Save yourself, family members and your pets the unpleasant experience of electrocution. Pay mind that there are no visible and open electrical wires which could cause a horrible shock by covering up exposed wires in the room with nifty, plastic guards you can purchase at your local hardware store.

Pay mind that strings from blinds or ropes from drapery are out of your playful Schnauzers reach because these could cause the dog to accidentally get it entangled whilst they are at play.

Chapter Four: Habitat Requirements

Store all vitamins and medications away, and high up in child-proofed closets and cabinets which are far from the reach of your Standard Schnauzer. Medicines, vitamins and herbal supplements made for human consumption are very dangerous to animals when ingested. Avoid this from happening to your young Schnauzer pup. Spare it from the discomfort, ill effects and an untimely visit to the vet.

Housing Temperature

Tips on How to Dog – Proof Your House

Keep in mind that one factor to keep your canine happy and content is to give it an environment and space where it is safe. As you make provisions for your new Standard Schnauzer make calculated, thoughtful measures as you prepare your home and yard area for your new canine's arrival and make sure that you remove any possible dangers to the new pet.

The innate curiosity of a dog becomes apparent when it is in new surroundings. Your Schnauzer will most certainly want to get their noses into each hidden nook and tucked away cranny of any new area with no regard for its safety. All your Schnauzer will be focused on is its quest for discovery - unless it gets a whiff of danger lurking. It will be up to you, as its new master, to refit and outfit your house to

Chapter Four: Habitat Requirements

meet a certain level of security so that your new Schnauzer dog is safe as it goes on pet-expeditions.

Make your house a safe environment for your new pet Schnauzer. Not only will thoughtful preparation do well for your new canine, it will also give you some peace of mind knowing that you have done everything which is necessary to make your home a safe place and secure fort for all.

Medication and pharmaceuticals, cleaning products, hair and body products, are items which are mostly made up of very toxic substances which can be quite dangerous to animals if they come into contact with or ingest these. To maintain a level of security and for your peace of mind, maintain an organized house and take the necessary measures of keeping your inquisitive canine away from these items.

- Secure and lock away all cleaning products, laundry and fabric softeners, bath soaps, body wash and shampoos, and all sorts of cleaning agents, away from where your Schnauzer's curiosity may take over get the better of it. Invest on and install child-proof locks on all your cabinet doors. These will not only prevent your prying pet from getting to these poisonous items - keeping cabinet doors closed and securely locked discourages your new pet from crawling into spaces

Chapter Four: Habitat Requirements

where it should not be in.

- Keep all sorts of food items out of your Schnauzer's reach by tightly securing food in tight, air-proof containers. Store uneaten food in the pantry or inside your refrigerator. This will not only discourage your pet from scrounging for food, you will also avoid the inconvenience of having to clean up mess created by your little buddy's curiosity.

- Securely fasten all rubbish bins with tight lids. Snug lids will not only keep rubbish and food left overs inside the bin; it will also keep your inquisitive little buddy out of a smelly mess.

- Make sure that all laundry chutes, washer and dryer doors are shut and locked. Your Schnauzer is a dog who enjoys exploring places and may get stuck or trapped in areas where it shouldn't be in in the first place. You have to check the inside of these places prior to using them should you forget to shut them.

- Keep toilet covers down when not in use. There is a high probability of your Schnauzer taking a drink of water from a bowl laden with chemicals which would be very dangerous and harmful for your dog. One other danger an open toilet bowl poses is the likelihood of your Schnauzer falling into the bowl. This can be a tough situation for your Schnauzer pup to get out of during the times it is left on its own.

- To discourage your Schnauzer from crawling into tight spaces it may have difficulty getting out of, block and cover areas or spaces your and will likely get into and where it may end up getting trapped.

The living room looks like an area safe enough because it is the common room where the family congregates. Because your new addition will be more likely to get into tight spots and places than the rest of the family, you will have to take caution and reassess your living room space.

- Should you have potted, indoor plants, you would primarily want to determine if these plants are safe and non-toxic to your Schnauzer. Toxic poisoning from chewing on leaves of plants is a very real Scenario. You want to remove these plants from the general spaces where your Schnauzer is allowed to freely roam. This not only avoids an accident of having the canine tip the plant over and creating a mess, but more so to avoid an avoidable trip to the vet.
- Remove all string, ropes, wires and electric cables or protect these with plastic wire covering. Exposed

Chapter Four: Habitat Requirements

electric cables and rope may get you Schnauzer entangled and cause it distress or worse. Electrical wires, when played with or chewed on can result in a nasty electric shock to your Schnauzer.

- Fragile curios, souvenirs, and breakable valuables have to be put away or stored in another room. Where they are away and out of the Schnauzer's line of sight or reach. Avoid accidents which may happen in case the Schnauzer gets too close for comfort.

Rooms

- Use a utility box to store away toys used by your Schnauzer. Toys with tiny parts or that can easily break may pose as a choking hazard to little toddlers and your new pet.

- Medicine, cosmetics, liquids in bottles and tubes, jewelry, keys, pills, and other small things your Schnauzer will be able to reach and play with are curiosities which it could gravitate to when it is in an exploratory mood. Save yourself the hassles of cleaning up after your inquisitive new addition, as well as the dread of finding out it had swallowed something it wasn't supposed to eat.

- Just like the wires in your living room, take pains that you utilize the same protective non-toxic, plastic coverings on any exposed wires to dissuade your new pet Schnauzer from chewing on a live wire. Cover all unused sockets that are unused for extra measure.

- Make sure that all cabinet doors are kept closed so that your Schnauzer doesn't crawl into one without being noticed. Nothing elevates stress levels than calling out for your pet only to find it hidden in an unsecured nook.

Backyard and Garage

These are the other more dangerous areas for your Schnauzer if they are allowed to play and roam in and inside these spaces within your home perimeter. If your Schnauzer has to spend time by itself whilst you are away at work, it will be wise to check and recheck these spaces for hazards it may come across.

- Make a mental note of the supplies you store in the garage. All paint cans, cleaning products, power tools, gas cans, etc. must be stored away from the dog's sight and fastened by doors with child-proof locks.

- Make certain that you do not leave out power tools, supplies and materials you are using for a project.

Chapter Four: Habitat Requirements

Take stock that all tools, equipment and implements are kept out of reach or locked away.

- Your Schnauzer will get into spaces that it may not be able to get out of by itself. Border up and cover all possible crawl spaces for an extra measure of safety.

- Check fences for holes your playful schnauzer may wiggle through. Not only can it hurt it while it forces its body through a gap, it is also a good way for a gateway and removed from the safety of its home.

- Before Stepping on the gas pedal check that your pet did not crawl under the car. This is an all too real scenario and one which has caused heartbreaks many times over. Before backing out, conduct a pet headcount. Call out loudly to your schnauzer/s and honk your horn to make sure it isn't camped out under the car.

Chapter Four: Habitat Requirements

Chapter Five: Nutrition and Feeding

Your Pet will always seem to be hungry and want more food and it will probably try anything and everything you offer it. It may even get into food not offered to it if food were left out where your voraciously eager eater can reach. A pet owner/guardian is warned to watch what foods are given to it to avoid obesity. We recommend free feeding your pet schnauzer only when it's young.

When your schnauzer first has its first solid meal until it is About 3 months old, free feeding is allowable to help it gain weight. This would also the best time to find out what sort of foods your schnauzer responds to with eagerness.

Chapter Five: Nutrition and Feeding

As you Progress toward the fourth month of solid foods, lessen the feeding frequency to 3 measured meals, given at regularly scheduled times of the day. Feeding outside of a schedule will work against and throw off house training your schnauzer.

Remember that training and teaching discipline at a young age, in all areas of your pet's life, is Crucial to a successful home life. Not only will schedule and disciplined grooming, feeding, and playtime help you factor all these activities into your weekly and daily routine, it will also have your canine be raised in a home where consistency is followed - resulting in a more even-mannered and socialized companion.

Nutritional Needs of Standard Schnauzer

The health and overall future well-being of your new schnauzer will depend greatly on the quality of food you give it. You, as give owner, have the Job of choosing the right kind of food which will provide your schnauzer all the elemental nutrients it requires to live a healthy life. Anticipate that you will have to experiment with different kinds of foods at the start until you figure out which nutritionally correct brand your schnauzer likes best before buying in bulk.

Chapter Five: Nutrition and Feeding

Food options are unlimited these days unlike times before when pet foods were few to choose from with such a Wide variety of selection to choose from, the job of choosing the right. Sorts of food for your schnauzer can be a difficult one if you do not know what your pet needs and what to avoid. This would be the best time to find out about the different ways manufacturers label their products and how these labels pave the way to identifying what foods, food additives and other whatnots pet food manufacturers put into their food mixes to make their products.

Talk to your vet about home and raw feeding your pet should you choose to go this route. Knowing the exact food requirements of your standard schnauzer dog is important to know because you will have a more active role in the buying, quality control, preparation and measurement ratios of the meals you will be serving it.

How to Select the Right Dog Food

We advise that you feed your Standard Schnauzer one to one-and-a-half cups of prime quality, premium dry dog food, divided into two scheduled meals. Make certain to choose a grain-free, veterinary-developed mix made in the U.S.A. Wheat, corn, and soy are fillers which provide no nutritional value and which can cause allergies and other

Chapter Five: Nutrition and Feeding

serious health issues. Also make sure that the food you choose for your standard Schnauzer does not have added sweeteners or sugar, and that is free of artificial colors, flavors, and preservatives.

The Standard Schnauzer has unique nutritional needs necessary for his overall health and wellbeing. Schnauzers are an active breed which requires real meat, with no by-products, listed first on the ingredient label to give enough protein to support its high energy level. Your schnauzer must also have a lot of whole fruits and vegetables to help enable its body to absorb important vitamins and nutrients from its food. A holistic, all-natural, antioxidant-rich formula has Omega-3 and Omega-6 fatty acids for the dog to have shiny coat and healthy skin. A good supply of Glucosamine gives way to optimum bone and joint development, which is crucial for a dog with this level of activity. Importantly, the best food for your Standard Schnauzer is one which is specifically made to meet the Schnauzer's individual needs.

Networking with a tight circle of seasoned Schnauzer owners, breeders and medical providers was previously mentioned within this book a few times for good reason having a close group of 'advisers' allows the sharing of pet food recipes, best practices, commercial food choices, and useful information for the new Schnauzer owner.

Chapter Five: Nutrition and Feeding

Be a thorough shopper, informed, and smart and learn to understand complicated ingredient names printed on manufacturer's labels. Get to know the truth behind labels which read 'meat by-product', 'by-products' or 'meal' since these are remains and odd parts of previously processed animal meats.

Canned pet foods are manufactured to be tasty to a dog's palate, easy to keep, and have very little preservatives added which is why canned foods have to be eaten soon after serving or it will spoil quickly. Canned pet foods are more expensive than dry pet foods but are an optimum choice for very young pups or a much older dog. Canned foods will have a higher concentration of water so your Schnauzer will probably require a larger portion if this is on the menu.

Dog foods that are semi-moist are chewier and are sold in bags of varied amounts. As compared to dry pet foods, semi-moist dog foods have a shorter shelf life. Pay mind that these foods contain sugar, to maintain the soft density of the food. This sort of foods frequently contains food coloring to make the food look more appealing. Some dogs have been seen to experience difficulties metabolizing these foods which result in softer stools and more frequent

Chapter Five: Nutrition and Feeding

bowel movements. This sort of pet food is not advisable to be given as main meals but rather, to be given as treats instead.

Another choice in the pet food market is the most affordable of all; kibble or commercially produced dry foods. Kibble or dry food, enjoys a longer shelf life as compared to wet or semi-moist dog foods. It has been noted to help avoid the buildup of plaque and tar in the dog's teeth. You must to employ your detection skills to decipher the labels on packages because many of the dry foods have additives and serve no nutritional value to your schnauzer. Keep in mind that you will find Varied choices of dog food products to pick from, with some better than most.

Raw feeding and home cooked meals are other options you could consider if you get too overwhelmed by the many choices out in the market. Talk to your vet if you choose to feed your Dog raw or home cooked food because you will have to mind measurements and portions and probably have to include vitamin supplements to complete a balanced dish each time.

Chapter Five: Nutrition and Feeding

Types of Commercial Dog Foods

Diet and nutrition is perhaps one of the most crucial decisions you will make for your pet schnauzer as it affects their immune system, long-term health, condition of their teeth, vital organs, coat and even their lifespan. So observe and find out and choose wisely.

Most pet owners are not "pet nutritionists" and are not aware about what to look for when they look at labels of foods. The truth is, there are a lot of brands out there to choose from and trying to select the optimum one with 100% certainty can be daunting and stressful. When picking a brand of pet food we recommend you base your choices on your pets breed, weight, age, gender, activity level. If they have any allergies or health issues to consider, keep those in mind too. If you need assistance or would like some advice about choosing the right kind of food for your Standard Schnauzers, get in touch with your Schnauzer society in your area or online.

You will discover during your research that there are many recommendations about what foods to feed, and not feed, your schnauzer. You will come across lots of commercial, marketing hype which you need to ignore. Understanding how to read and figuring out food labels and what ingredients, additives and extenders are used in the mix is an ability you will need to develop.

Chapter Five: Nutrition and Feeding

In order to give their product mass, volume and flavor, store bought foods made by canine food manufacturers, use extenders like corn and soy which give the food no nutritional value and could result in allergies to your canines. A lot of these dog foods also have meat by-products mixed in them. These are animal parts which were unused and previously rejected. These are parts and portions of processed animal meat meant for the consumption of people. These are parts like, pig nose, cow hoof, fatty and bony parts of chicken, ears, parts of the animal's face, and even road kill.

Picking out a high-quality canine food product for your Schnauzer can be tricky since there are a lot of different options out in the market. You can trim down your choices, however, by choosing a size-specific product – a formula for small-breed Miniature Schnauzers, a formula for medium breed Standard Schnauzers, and a formula for large-breed Giant Schnauzers. You will find some reviews below on some of the selected prime-quality canine food mixes we found that could be good food choices and alternatives for your Schnauzer:

Natural Balance LID Lamb & Rice Small Breed Recipe –
This dog food product is made with prime ingredients in a healthy, balanced mixture. This Natural

Chapter Five: Nutrition and Feeding

Balance LID Lamb & Rice Small Breed Recipe is a perfect choice for dogs which are small-breeds like the Miniature Schnauzer. The recipe uses lamb meal as the food's primary source of protein along with brown and white rice as digestible carbohydrates. This recipe gives a balance of important and essential fatty acids which is good for your dog's skin and fur. It also provides a concentrated source of energy. This recipe is made to support your Schnauzer's digestive health while helping it maintain a healthy bodyweight. In addition it has healthy supplements which include a variety of vitamins and several chelated minerals. In a nutshell, this recipe will satisfy your small-breed dog's nutritional requirements and satiate its cravings for natural flavor.

Merrick Grain-Free LID Salmon & Sweet Potato Recipe

This prime-quality, grain-free diet will not aggravate your Schnauzer food sensitivities or allergies. Should your canine suffer from dog allergies consider this product brand, Merrick Grain-Free LID Salmon & Sweet Potato Recipe. This recipe has deboned salmon, sweet potatoes, salmon meal, potatoes and peas, as the top 5 ingredients that will give you the confidence knowing that your dog's protein requirements are met. It has plenty of supplements like crucial vitamins and healthy minerals which gives the dog nutritional balance. This recipe also has a lot of natural

Chapter Five: Nutrition and Feeding

flavors which will appeal to your Schnauzer. Since this recipe is not just formulated for dogs of a specific size, it can be a wise choice for a Standard Schnauzer who can be anywhere between medium to large size breed. Just make certain that you follow the recommendations for feeding on the package in order to determine the amount of food you should feed to your Schnauzer according to its body weight and activity level.

Blue Buffalo Basics Large Breed Adult Lamb & Potato Recipe

This is a good choice if you are in search of a high-quality canine food made especially for dogs that are of the large-breed like the Giant Schnauzer. The product also takes into consideration the risk for food allergies in dogs. The Blue Buffalo Basics Large Breed Adult Lamb & Potato Recipe is a great option to consider for your big Standard Schnauzer or a Giant Schnauzer. This recipe is primarily made up of protein-rich lamb used as the only source of protein mixed with peas and potatoes for gluten- and grain-free carbohydrate needs. Since this recipe is produced with a just a few quality ingredients, it will surely meet your canine's nutritional needs without setting off its food allergies or sensitivities. In addition, the food is supplemented with omega fatty acids for good skin promotion and coat health. It also has an exact blend of

Chapter Five: Nutrition and Feeding

phosphorus as well as calcium to promote strong bones and teeth. This Blue Buffalo's Life Source Bits recipe features a mix of specially blended nutrients to increase your dog's immune health and to provide optimum nutritional balance.

Toxic Foods to Avoid

As a responsible Standard Schnauzer owner, you need to keep in mind that not all foods and drinks are suitable food your Standard Schnauzer's diet. There are many food items which, if your pet gets into, could cause it a great deal of harm, an unexpected emergency visit to the vet or much worse. Yes, there is food that if your Schnauzer ingests could pose a mountain of medical problems. You will be doing the right thing on finding out what sort of foods your Schnauzer should not be eating. We have compiled a list of foods which are generally considered a "no-go" for most canines and are true for your new pet as well.

Keep macadamia nuts out of the reach of your Standard Schnauzer because if it does manage to get to these nuts it will cause muscle tremors, weakness and vomiting in most if not all dogs.

When walnuts become infected with mold and fungus after a spell of rain produces harmful toxins which if ingested can cause great harm and make your Standard

Chapter Five: Nutrition and Feeding

horribly sick and possibly die. You don't want this to happen because the signs are awfully horrible what with trembling, drooling, lethargy, lack of coordination, vomiting, loss of appetite, along with indications of jaundice accompanied by yellow gums and eyes. Keep this food product lidded tightly, up and away from the reach of your inquisitive Schnauzer.

You may have seen pictures of dogs on the Internet where it seemed inebriated, looking foolishly drunk beside a bottle of alcohol. Yes, it may seem funny and amusing at first, but believe you me, it isn't a laughing matter. Dogs can get seriously ill with alcohol poisoning and when it happens it will be a cause of great concern. Keep all alcohol away from your dogs and make sure that no one attempts to have it drink up. Be mindful of your dogs during parties. Keep in mind that dogs, most especially your Schnauzer, are inquisitive explorers and may get a drink or two in without you noticing.

Who doesn't love onions or garlic in their food? These are usual ingredients humans use often to spice up their food, but beware that your Schnauzer not gets into these. If and when ingested by dogs, onions and garlic will affect the red blood cell count of the canine negatively.

You want to make sure that any meats fed to your Schnauzer are free of tiny bones. Bones crushed by the

Chapter Five: Nutrition and Feeding

strong teeth of a canine still pose a threat to them and a dangerous one indeed. Bones tend to break up and splinter in shards. Bits of bones will cause blockages and intestinal perforations and could lacerate your dog's tongue, throat and intestines. Bones could also damage the teeth of your Schnauzer.

We humans consume so much food and prepare so much of it that we usually are left with leftover food. First of all not all foods fit for human consumption is good for dogs. In fact most of it, because of the spices, salt and sugars we add to them, are bad for dogs. On top of that, spoilt food which is moldy doubles the repercussions to a dog when ingested. Spoilt and moldy human leftovers or even their own special foods will cause grave illness in the dog. A canine can get ill from them and start showing these signs through seizing, vomiting, tremors, diarrhea and sadly death.

Coffee products and coffee based drinks or foods are toxic substances which affect a canine's nervous system and heart. It causes seizures, tremors, vomiting, increased and irregular heartbeat, diarrhea, fever, coma and death.

Chocolates cause adverse reactions and effects to all dogs and must be totally avoided. The signs may not become apparent immediately but when it does it will be a regrettable time and a sorry sight. Keep your dog away from chocolates at all costs.

Fruit pits of peaches, apricots, cherries and plums have cyanogenic glycosides, which when ingested causes cyanide poisoning. A very scary thought indeed if you consider the consequences. What you want to do instead is slice fruit up and gives it to your dog sans the pit. As a rule of thumb, keep away all fruit pits from the food of your dog!

Tips in Feeding Your Standard Schnauzer

What dog doesn't enjoy a slab of juicy meat? However, you still want to make sure that your Standard Schnauzer gets a balanced meal regularly so that it gets properly nourished. Schnauzers are great, active players and will have a seemingly endless supply of energy so they will eat heartily each time. Make sure that you teach and instill discipline early on so they have proper eating habits.

Always schedule feeding as this will teach your Schnauzers discipline as this is also a part of their socialization training. You wouldn't want your Schnauzer to run off and ingest the first sign of "food" it detects whenever and wherever. Observe a level of consistency with your Schnauzers because this is will allow you to raise an even-mannered canine companion.

Chapter Six: Grooming and Training Your Standard Schnauzer

The standard Schnauzer has a double coat consisting of a lush, soft undercoat and a harsh, wiry topcoat. Loose, dead hair which normally sheds off has a tendency to get trapped under all that lush fur so Schnauzers are generally considered good pets for those which allergies and asthma who have little tolerance for loose, shedding fur.

The trademark look of the Schnauzer with its be-moustache facial hair is a look most owners like to maintain hence they prefer to only trim areas of their Schnauzers body like the head, neck, ears, chest and stomach, allowing the hair on its legs to grow on the legs and face only - keeping

Chapter Six: Grooming and Training Your Schnauzer

with its distinct bearded look. Nail trimming is also a must for Schnauzers.

Grooming Needs

Your standard Schnauzer will need to get regular grooming every five to eight weeks. Most Schnauzer owners opt to employ the services of a professional groomer, because properly clipping the nails of an active Schnauzer can be tricky. Show dogs are hand-stripped, a time consuming process involving "ripping" the coat of the Schnauzer by hand, and is not a necessary grooming detail for dogs that will not be shown. It is crucial that you as owner brush your Schnauzer two to three times per week in order to prevent matting and tangling of its coat. As with all canines, and because they eat every day, the beard needs cleaning and grooming every day.

Check your Standard Schnauzer's ears regularly for indications of wax buildup, infection or irritation. Use a cotton ball moistened with a vet-approved cleaner during downtime when your Schnauzer is tuckered out and relaxed. Brush its teeth on a weekly basis as this staves off plaque buildup and keeps bad breath at bay. Monthly trimming of nails is recommended if these done trim down naturally.

Chapter Six: Grooming and Training Your Schnauzer

Your Schnauzer will need attentive brushing and grooming to maintain its coarse, harsh and wiry coat. Daily brushing also promotes proper distribution of essential skin oils to its skin. You will need to get a good and strong brush and pick up a reliable vacuum from the store. Don't hold back and scrimp on these sundries because you and your Schnauzer will be using these for a long time to come.

Training and Dealing with Your Dog's Behavior

Teaching any skill at an early age gives a student the advantage of gaining higher intelligence as it hones its good attributes and curbs its bad ones. Early training allows any student to fare better in life especially with regard to social interactions.

Standard Schnauzers are innately wary of strangers and will sound off the minute it detects danger or an unfamiliar presence in its midst. Being in new situations will also bring about this reaction. Being in new environments can cause the canine to display excessive excitement or unnecessary anxiety. Curb these behavioral traits by making sure that the pup is coming from even tempered parents and that was born out of proper breeding methods overseen by an upstanding breeder. Next, introduce your Schnauzer to obedience training whilst it is young works well to its advantage. Avert these behavioral issues and channel traits of misgivings in a good way by bringing your Schnauzer to places where it can freely roam under attentively watchful eye.

Be patient with your young Schnauzer as it gets to know about new places, faces and spaces. Give it a chance to get acquainted with what it sees as unusual and different and allow it to grab footing. Give it the edge and begin obedience training at a young age. Not only will it learn the niceties of canine manners it will also give him an edge on getting used to the company of an assortment of people as well as other canines alike.

Training Tips for Your Standard Schnauzers

A would-be guardian needs to introduce the canine to a variety of situations so that the canine is exposed to different situations and scenarios. This is how a dog begins its socialization training. Early socialization promotes the good traits of dogs and they are likelier to become well behaved as they mature. Allow your dog to gain familiarity of various situations in order for it to gain good footing in life.

The early stages of puppyhood are the best time to start out your canine on training and socialization.

Chapter Six: Grooming and Training Your Schnauzer

Introduction to socialization and behavioral training at an early age allows your Schnauzer pet to grow up applying what it has learnt in everyday situations. This not only gives your Schnauzer puppy the edge of becoming more friendly and effective as its good traits are honed and not-so-desirable traits are toned down, early training also allows it to get ready for its debut to situations and environments beyond the home and yard. Training it whilst it is young also teaches your Schnauzer pup social manners as it improves the innate traits it was originally bred for.

Housebreaking Tips for your Standard Schnauzers

Invest on a strong, sturdy dog crate which your Schnauzer will be using for a long time. Not only is it an ingenious method of house training your Schnauzer puppy, it also helps to train them to stay relaxed and happy during separation from their guardians. This is highly advisable for Schnauzers who may experience a bit of anxiety when left on its own.

Make it a point to give each dog delegated areas in the house to retreat to when all tuckered out from a day of romping. Place its crate in a relatively hidden but interactive area of the home like a hallway or under an indoor planter. Give space provisions for your Schnauzer where it can eat in

Chapter Six: Grooming and Training Your Schnauzer

peace and enjoy its meals. Provide your Schnauzer its own space in the family kitchen and allocate an area where it can eat its meals in solitude. Invest on and choose slow-feeding bowls so your Schnauzer is discouraged from wolfing down its food too fast. Buy the stainless steel kind of feeding bowl because this will less likely deteriorate with extended use.

Chapter Seven: Showing Your Schnauzers

Your Standard Schnauzer is one of the most intelligent dogs of the canine spectrum and a highly competent working dog at that which gives assistance in many areas of human society. From being one-time ratters and guard dogs, they have moved up in the working class group of canines to become therapy dogs, and assistant to the disabled. They have flanked the sides of military and police personnel. They are excellent trackers and detection canines used to sniff out illegal substances and deadly bombs.

Chapter Seven: Showing Your Schnauzers

It wouldn't be a surprise if you wanted to show off your Schnauzers skills and abilities to the world. We shall discuss the standard breed of Schnauzers in this chapter and reveal what is required for them to enter.

For Schnauzer Dog Breed Standard

A robust, strongly built dog and with plenty of bone and good muscle structure, the Standard schnauzer is a heavy set dog. It is proportional in body length and height and is squarely built. It has a harsh, dense coat of fur which is accentuated by the breed hallmark with eyebrows that are arched and bristly whiskers and moustache. Any deviation from these physical traits is considered to be faults and is penalized according to the deviation extent.

PROPORTION, SUBSTANCE, SIZE

18.5 to 19.5 inches is the ideal height from the highest point of the male Schnauzers shoulder blades. 17.5 to 18.5 inches is the ideal height from highest point of the shoulder blades for females. Deviation from these specifications is faulted in relation to the extent of difference. Any dog measuring under or over half an inch is disqualified. The shoulder blades at its highest point are the sum of distance from breastbone to end of the rump.

HEAD

The Schnauzers head is to be rectangular, strong and long. It is to narrow slightly from ears to eyes and to tip of nose. The length of the head in total is around half the length at the back from the shoulder blades down to its tail. Its head is to match the dog's gender and substance. Its expression is spirited, alert and intelligent. Its oval in shaped eyes is to be medium sized, dark brown, trained forward. Eyes should neither be round or be protruded. Its brow should be wiry and arched without impeding the dog's vision. Brows must not be too long that it hides the canine's eyes. Its ears are to be evenly shaped, set high with adequate leather thickness and sported erect. If uncropped, ears are to be medium sized and v-shaped and mobile in order that ears break at cranium level. They are to be carried forward and inner edges close to its cheeks. The dog is faulted for showing hound-like ears.

SKULL

The skull from occiput to stop is to be slightly wide from ear to ear and the skull width measurement should not exceed the skull length by two thirds. Its skull is to be flat, not bumpy or domed. Skin on its face is to be unwrinkled and taut with a moderate stop accentuated by its wiry brows. Its muzzle is both equal and parallel to the length of the tip of its skull and must be strong. The muzzle is to end in a blunt, slight wedge with its wiry whiskers accentuating the shape of its rectangular cranium. The upper part of its muzzle is to be parallel to the skull's top line. Its nose is to be black, full and large. Its lips are not to overlap; they are to be tight and black in colour. It has to have properly developed chewing cheek muscles but not overly so that it interrupts the rectangular form of its head.

BITE

The Schnauzers mouth should display a full set of pearly white teeth that are strong, with good scissor bite. The dogs should be pristinely developed with upper incisors mildly overlapping as it engages the lower incisors. Its lower and upper jaws are to be powerful; not overshot or undershot. The candidate is faulted if the bite is level because it is undesirable however its faulted less than an undershot or overshot bite.

Chapter Seven: Showing Your Schnauzers

NECK, TOPLINE, BODY

The neck of the canine is shown strong, with balanced length and thickness. It is elegantly arched and blends in cleanly into its shoulders. Its skin is taut, fits close to its dry throat sans dewlaps or wrinkles. The upper back is not be utterly horizontal, but must have a slight descent in slant which begins at the drop of the primary vertebra to a croup slightly curved and attached to its tail. The Schnauzers back is to show short, straight, firm and strong. Its loin is to be well developed, and there must be a small distance of space between the last ribs to the hips.

BODY

The Schnauzer's body is to be short-coupled, strong, compact, as well as substantial, to allow complete agility and flexibility. Faults are found when body is too slender, skinny, coarse or bulky. Its medium width chest should have well-formed ribs, and can be seen as oval shaped across. The dog's breastbone is to be clearly seen. Its brisket has to gradually slope downward to its elbows and gradually ascend toward the back of the dog with a slightly drawn up belly. Faulted if found tucked-up excessively or if it's rump is full or slightly rounded. The canine's tail is to be slight;y set high and straight. It is to be docked not more than two

Chapter Seven: Showing Your Schnauzers

inches or less than one inch or faulted for a bushy, squirrel-like tail.

FRONT LEGS

Its shoulder blades are sloped and strongly muscled, but even and proportionately placed that the curved higher ends are nearly vertical in line above its elbows. Shoulders should be sloped forward where they are joined to the fore arm, assembled at a right angle as closely as possible when observed from the side. This angulation allows the ultimate onward continuation of its forelegs sans difficulty or struggle. Its front legs are to show vertical and straight, sans traces of curvature when observed from any angle; they are set slightly far apart; heavy boned; its elbows are close to the canine's frame and trained to its back. The fifth nail on its forelegs can be removed. Its feet should be compact and small, circular and with padded thickly as well as sturdy ebony nails. Its toes are to be arched and well closed and pointed straight ahead.

HINDQUARTERS

Back legs are to be strongly muscled and equal with the front legs, they are not to appear higher than its shoulders. Its thighs are wide with stifles well bent. Its lower

Chapter Seven: Showing Your Schnauzers

legs, from knee to ankles, should approximately be equal extending to the dog's highest neckline point. Its legs, starting at the visibly clear ankle up to its paws, are brief and horizontal to the floor. When observed from the back they are to be even with the front legs. The fifth claw on the back legs can be clipped and both front and back feet should be the same.

COAT

Its coat is to be tight, tough, wiry and lush, made up of a supple, close to skin undercoat and a wiry outer coating which, when observed at right angles sticks out off its back and not lying smooth or flat. Its outer fur is to be plucked out, so the body outline is emphasized. Since the texture of the coat is very important, a dog could be classified in show coat if back hair length is measured at 3/4 to 2 inches. The coat on its belly area, chest, neck, head, ears and under its tail must be trimmed closely so it has the appearance typical of Standards. Coat on its snout and above its eyes is to be lengthened to form its distinct eyebrows and beard; Fur on its legs should be longer than the hair on the frame. Fur must have a wiry texture and must not be too profuse to take away its clean look or capabilities to work of the canine. Faults are found if coat is too shaggy, soft, curly, wavy, or smooth; if it is too short or too long; if undercoat too scant or lacking; faulted for excessive or furnishings that are lacking.

COAT COLOR

All Black or Salt and Pepper - the usual black and white color of the canine's outer fur is the outcome of the combination of ebony and albino hairs; black hairs tangled with white. All hues of salt and pepper as well as ashen to silver-stone are acceptable, perfect salt and pepper Standards have an ashen lower coat. However a light brown or yellowish tan lower coat is not to be faulted. The canine is acceptable to sport a deeper colored face which blends with the specific hue of the topcoat. In salt and pepper dogs, the salt and pepper blend could lighten to lighter ash or silver, albino-white around its brows, under throat, whiskers, across its chest, cheeks, beneath its tail, leg colors, underbody, and inner legs.

Ideally ebony - colored Schnauzers must be a real rich color, sans any hazy or discoloration that neither pales out; nor should there be any tan or gray hairs. Its undercoat must also be ebony-black. But, advanced age or extreme sun exposure may result to some hazy discoloration. It is not a fault if a tiny white patch is found on its chest. Color loss of due to scars from bites and nicks is not penalized or faulted.

Chapter Seven: Showing Your Schnauzers

Colors apart from what is specified are deducted points as well as any mixtures or shadings found in the topcoat like red, rust, yellow, brown, fawn or tan; A Standard is faulted when there is absence of peppering, spotting or striping, when a streak of black is apparent down its back, or a saddle of black absent of usual white and black hairs, ashen fur amongst a black coat; lastly, in ebony-colored Standards, all lower fur colors other than black.

GAIT

The canine is to show a quick, free, sound, strong, real and balanced gait using strong, properly proportioned back legs which span out and travel good ground. Its front legs must reach out in a stride mirroring its back legs. When in trot, its back is to remain solid, strong and balanced, absent of sway, curling or overreaching. Previewed from the back, all four legs, although these could appear to be near each other when in trot, is not to crossover or hit each other. It is to display increased speed causing all four legs to meet at the gravity's middle line.

TEMPER

The Schnauzer possesses extremely good faculties, able to learn quickly, intelligence, endurance, fearlessness,

Chapter Seven: Showing Your Schnauzers

and has good tolerance for all weathers and sickness. Its nature is a combination of having an energetic enthusiasm with utter dependability.

FAULTS

In determining the gravity of a flaw, utmost consideration must be considered to divergence from the required spirited, highly intelligent, alert, reliable character traits of the Schnauzer. Schnauzers which are bashful or seem extremely nervous must be gravely penalized and excused from competing. Disqualification is meted for vicious dogs.

Chapter Eight: Breeding Your Schnauzer

Schnauzer breeders have long realized and discovered the secrets of successful Schnauzer breeding and our aim is to impart these with you here. Whilst making a good match for these adorable canines is the same to breeding dogs in general, you want to take careful steps to ensure a safe and successful pairing. When breeding Schnauzers correctly, you help to bring forth new puppies into the world so make certain you are ready for that responsibility before you begin.

Chapter Eight: Breeding Your Schnauzer

Breeding Basics

Select a perfect breeding pair. Get in touch with and network with upstanding and recently successful breeders as well as your trusted vet to locate a good sire and bitch pair. If your own Schnauzers come from different parent, you may use them as well. Again, it is highly advisable to work with seasoned and upstanding breeders as they would have better experience in making decisions about what makes a good pairing. You want to determine and make sure that both sire and bitch are in good health, registered and have pleasant personality traits before you begin breeding.

When the time is right and perfect, place both male (sire) and female (bitch) Schnauzers in the same enclosure, preferably outdoors. Be mindful of the mating activity. If and once the dogs begin mating the process usually lasts up to 45 minutes.

You have to first keep in mind that you need to keep the female healthy. Pregnancy is challenging for female dogs. This is especially true for smaller Schnauzer breeds. So, do work closely with your vet to make sure that she and her puppies are kept healthy.

Chapter Eight: Breeding Your Schnauzer

Wait until the female is fertile. The Schnauzer bitch primarily needs to be "in heat." All female canines experience their cycles twice a year. This heat period lasts for about 21 days however she will not be fertile for the entire time. When her discharge is clear this indicates that the fertile period is about to begin. This usually happens 10 to 14 days after her cycle starts.

Keep the female away from the male dogs. Female dogs in heat attract male attention and aggressive males may attack or injure the female by attempting to mate with her before she is ready to mate. Male dogs can also impregnate her and ruin the litter purity. Keep in mind that unlike us humans, female canines can have multiple fathers in a single puppy litter. Make use of a secure kennel to keep male in and away from the females. Keep females in separate and enclosed kennels to prevent her from escaping to find a mate on her own.

Check for her fertility because you don't want to start breeding canines before the female is ready and fertile or she will resist the male. Make sure the female is fertile and visit your vet as your vet would be the best person able to check her hormone levels. You can also try scratching the base of her tail and if she lifts her tail and wags it side to side this indicates her readiness. This "flagging" motion is thought to be a way to beckon prospective dogs.

Be present and watch the birth. The outcome of a successful Schnauzer breeding shall result in a healthy litter anywhere between 61 to 64 days after the mating. Place a whelping box where the female Schnauzer can be comfortable during and after the birth of her puppies. Keep track and be mindful of the expected date of the birth so that you or another family member or adult caregiver is there and available to assist in case of complications.

Exercise patience because you will have to wait because you won't know if puppies will be a result of the pairing for at least a month. False pregnancy can also give the same indication such as engorged nipples and considerable weight gain. The way you can tell for sure if your bitch is indeed pregnant is to have it undergo an ultrasound a month after the pairing, to say if she is indeed pregnant.

Raising Puppies

Be ready for a whole lot of active fun and rambunctious play once your female Schnauzer gives birth because it will be a full house indeed! Raising Schnauzer

Chapter Eight: Breeding Your Schnauzer

puppies isn't exactly a walk in the park but it isn't too hard either given their minimal chances for acquiring illness. As long as they are carefully taken care of, given optimum feeding ratios with the right balance of food, they will be happy campers who would gather at your feet the minute they get a whiff of you at the driveway.

Brace yourself for an actively playful bunch that will be curious little beings that do not seem to get enough of exploring the world around them. They are a little stubborn and mischievous in their ways and you would not want to miss out on these formative months when they are the most inquisitive and the sponge-like in imbibing the teachings imparted to them. Starting off Schnauzers on obedience training is the way you would want to go at this point because this is the best time when they learn and unlearn stuff that would give them the best advantage of living full lives, able to be around many things and ready to experience new things, places and people.

They are best suited to be paired with families with young children, who are taught to treat animals with reverence and respect. Standard Schnauzers are also affectionately good companions to active seniors and single people. They are best suited to live with families, couples or individuals who have ample yard space where they can play

Chapter Eight: Breeding Your Schnauzer

and explore to their hearts content. They are also likely and very apt candidates for farm-life living where they can be utilized as ratters, herders but most of all security dogs who will be loyal companions for a long, long time.

Chapter Nine: Common Illnesses of Schnauzer Dogs

The Standard Schnauzer has very little health concerns but it is nonetheless recommended that they, especially those who are used for breeding, have radiography procedures done to clear then of hip dysplasia. There are available records at the Orthopedic Foundation for Animals which keep record animals which are purebred and have given the clear for hip dysplasia.

Chapter Nine: Common Illnesses of Schnauzer Dogs

It is also advised that Standard Schnauzers get annually tested for eye disease. Remember that when purchasing a Schnauzer from a breeder, they are to hand over certificates clearing the parents of the pup from hip dysplasia and eye disease. You will be able to minimize any health issues in your dog as long as you feed it the proper balanced diet it needs, keep its enclosure clean and maintained, and giving it the proper amount of exercise and activity time it needs.

You will want to minimize outdoor forays on hot or humid days. You will want to have it stay comfortably indoors in an environment of regulated air-conditioning during hot spells. You will have to use a leash when you and your Schnauzer go out for walks. Think about using a Y-shaped harness instead which goes around the Schnauzers chest instead of its throat. A collar wrapped around its neck makes it harder for any dog to breathe because this may put pressure on its windpipe.

Make it a habit to wash and dry the face and neck of the Schnauzer thoroughly and completely after each meal - much like you would yourself or your child after eating. This ensures that the dog is kept clean at all times preventing any food particles from staying on its skin which could lead to skin infections and rashes.

Chapter Nine: Common Illnesses of Schnauzer Dogs

Minor Problems:

Ticks and fleas are always a problem for all animals, be them wild or domestic ones. Your Schnauzer is at an advantage because it has you to check for these things in its body. Make sure that you use bathing products fit for animals sans dangerous chemicals which may cause it more harm than good. Never attempt to use human shampoo or soap on your pets.

Major Problems:

The Schnauzer is a fairly healthy canine and has very little medical concerns. As long as you take heed and pay mind to the people you will be dealing with - in other words, the breeders - you and the canine should not have much to worry about in terms of its physical health. Hip dysplasia is commonly found in Schnauzers who have not been bred using proper methods. This is an inherited medical condition which can be avoided if you deal with the right sort of breeders.

Another medical issue it suffers - also inherited and passed down by unhealthy parents - is eye disease. Make sure that the canine pup you acquire comes from mindful breeders who only employ the approved methods of

Chapter Nine: Common Illnesses of Schnauzer Dogs

procreation. Do not forget to claim the certificates from the OFA and from the breeders freeing and clearing the canine pup's parents from these medical conditions.

Vaccinations for Puppies and Adult Dogs

There are no arguments that dogs need vaccinations and how these preventative measures ensure a better life for our canine buddies. However, vaccinating your dog at the wrong time could spell disaster for the dog's health. Never vaccinate a weak dog.

Vaccines could also cause a great amount of stress to our canine's immune system and is said to greatly contribute to chronic diseases in canines. Over vaccinating a dog could cause it more harm than good especially if done without regard for the future well - being of the animal.

It has been proven that vaccinations prevent more serious illnesses from plaguing out pets but it should be done with restraint and thoughtful care

Chapter Nine: Common Illnesses of Schnauzer Dogs

Vaccination Schedule

When the animal's immune system is developing, it is the most vulnerable to the stresses of vaccines. Wait until the animal is at least 12 weeks old and only vaccinate against the most urgent medical conditions. Booster shots are mostly contended in the medical realm and you should ask questions about the advantages of booster shots if your vet recommends them to your canine.

First Aid Treatments

We should not play vet/doctor to our Schnauzers when grave medical cases arise, however, as with other humans, we should have a measure of knowledge on giving first aid to our loved ones when needed.

Here is a compilation of things you need to remember in case of emergency:
- surgical gloves
- styptic powder
- hydrogen peroxide
- eyewash solution
- vaseline/ lubricant jelly
- antiseptic wipes

Chapter Nine: Common Illnesses of Schnauzer Dogs

- instant cold compress (gel packs)
- instant hot compress
- alcohol swabs (to sterilize) antibiotic ointment for non-puncture wounds
- gauze pads
- adhesive tape
- tweezers
- syringes
- scissors
- rectal thermometer
- cotton balls
- towel

You first need to gather appropriate first aid supplies and build up a first aid kit for your canine. On this box, you should have the number of your veterinarian, just in case someone else in the family chances upon the emergency.

Conclusion

Now that you have come to the end of this book, you have done all the research you needed to learn about the Standard Schnauzer. You are now more than ever close to readiness in receiving your new Schnauzer.

You are lucky to be waiting for a fairly healthy breed sort with very few medical conditions. We encourage you to look into rescue and adoption before considering buying a Schnauzer. You must look for reputable breeders with recent success in breeding and ask all pertinent questions about the animal. When dealing with upstanding breeders you will be handed over some papers including receipt of down payment, full payment, medical and historical records of both parents and puppy, medical notations of vaccinations received and done, any treatments it may have undergone as well as clean bills of health from the OFA.

Keep in mind that maintaining its good health constitutes the maintenance of cage, crate, enclosure and living space, optimal food choices which give it a balanced diet with all nutrients present in its food. You want to spend time with it and engage your Schnauzer with mental and physical activities to keep it sharp, active and happy. You must have the puppy go to obedience training as early as possible in order for it to hone its skills and abilities and to get rid of any behavioral problems it may display.

What is left now is to wait for your Schnauzer to join you and your loved ones. Meeting your Schnauzer will be a joyous time and we hope that you have a great relationship with your new companion. As a parting and friendly reminder, we want to have you keep in mind that. as with us humans, Schnauzers too possess their own individual traits and personalities, hence we encourage you to spend good quality time with your new pet and get to know it well.

Photo Credits

Page 1 Photo by user 3816258 via Pixabay.com, https://pixabay.com/en/dogs-schnauzer-hay-bales-1847816/

Page 9 Photo by user IsabellWolf via Pixabay.com, https://pixabay.com/en/miniature-schnauzer-black-dog-1923470/

Page 31 Photo by user Kaz via Pixabay.com, https://pixabay.com/en/schnauzer-miniature-schnauzer-dog-275936/

Page 42 Photo by user kim_hester via Pixabay.com, https://pixabay.com/en/dog-heide-grass-schnauzer-puppy-1785748/

Page 53 Photo by user paula_mondragon via Pixabay.com, https://pixabay.com/en/schnauzer-dog-pet-animal-friend-1150228/

Page 66 Photo by user todabasura via Pixabay.com, https://pixabay.com/en/dog-pet-schnauzer-animal-domestic-1053662/

Page 72 Photo by user skeeze via Pixabay.com, https://pixabay.com/en/schnauzer-dog-canine-domestic-893171/

Page 83 Photo by user Shelleyknows via Pixabay.com, https://pixabay.com/en/dogs-schnauzer-pet-dog-breed-1548707/

Page 89 Photo by user 825545 via Pixabay.com, https://pixabay.com/en/funny-hybrid-wuschelig-schnauzer-mix-750599/

Page 95 Photo by user Adrain via Pixabay.com, https://pixabay.com/en/dog-park-woods-schnauzer-fashion-1917594/

References

"About Buying a Dog" AKC.org

http://www.akc.org/dog-owners/future-dog-owner/about-buying-a-dog/

"About Dog Vaccines" Schnauzers-Rule.com

http://www.schnauzers-rule.com/dog-vaccines.html

"AKC Official Breed Standard for the Standard Schnauzer" StandardSchnauzer.org

http://www.standardschnauzer.org/breed_standard.htm

"Bad Foods for Dogs" Schnauzers-Rule.com

http://www.schnauzers-rule.com/bad-foods.html

"Breed Information about the Standard Schnauzer" StandardSchnauzer.org

http://www.standardschnauzer.org/breed_info.htm

"Dog Crate Training" Dogtime.com

http://dogtime.com/dog-health/general/364-housetraining-crate-training

"How to Breed Schnauzer" Cuteness.com

https://www.cuteness.com/article/breed-schnauzer

"Prepare a Dog First Aid Kit" Schnauzers-Rule.com
http://www.schnauzers-rule.com/dog-first-aid.html

"Standard Schnauzer" Dogtime.com

http://dogtime.com/dog-breeds/standard-schnauzer#/slide/1

"Standard Schnauzer" PetGuide.com

http://www.petguide.com/breeds/dog/standard-schnauzer

"Standard Schnauzer" Wikipedia.com

https://en.wikipedia.org/wiki/Standard_Schnauzer

"Standard Schnauzer: Mittelschnauzer, Schnauzer, and Wirehair Pinscher" PetBreeds.com

http://dogs.petbreeds.com/l/149/Standard-Schnauzer

"United States Pet Passport Regulations (excluding Hawaii)" PetTravel.com
http://www.pettravel.com/immigration/UnitedStates.cfm

"What Dog is Right for Me" AKC.org
http://www.akc.org/dog-owners/future-dog-owner/find-breed/

"Your Schnauzer's Veterinarian" Schnauzers-Rule.com
http://www.schnauzers-rule.com/veterinarian.ht

Feeding Baby
Cynthia Cherry
978-1941070000

Axolotl
Lolly Brown
978-0989658430

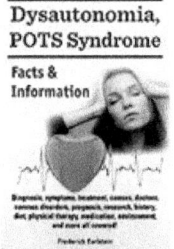

Dysautonomia, POTS
Syndrome
Frederick Earlstein
978-0989658485

Degenerative Disc
Disease Explained
Frederick Earlstein
978-0989658485

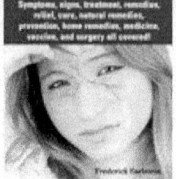

Sinusitis, Hay Fever,
Allergic Rhinitis Explained
Frederick Earlstein
978-1941070024

Wicca
Riley Star
978-1941070130

Zombie Apocalypse
Rex Cutty
978-1941070154

Capybara
Lolly Brown
978-1941070062

Eels As Pets
Lolly Brown
978-1941070167

Scabies and Lice Explained
Frederick Earlstein
978-1941070017

Saltwater Fish As Pets
Lolly Brown
978-0989658461

Torticollis Explained
Frederick Earlstein
978-1941070055

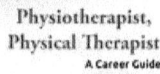

Kennel Cough
Lolly Brown
978-0989658409

Physiotherapist, Physical Therapist
Christopher Wright
978-0989658492

Rats, Mice, and Dormice As Pets
Lolly Brown
978-1941070079

Wallaby and Wallaroo Care
Lolly Brown
978-1941070031

Bodybuilding Supplements
Explained
Jon Shelton
978-1941070239

Demonology
Riley Star
978-19401070314

Pigeon Racing
Lolly Brown
978-1941070307

Dwarf Hamster
Lolly Brown
978-1941070390

Cryptozoology
Rex Cutty
978-1941070406

Eye Strain
Frederick Earlstein
978-1941070369

Inez The Miniature Elephant
Asher Ray
978-1941070353

Vampire Apocalypse
Rex Cutty
978-1941070321

www.ingramcontent.com/pod-product-compliance
Lightning Source LLC
LaVergne TN
LVHW051657080426
835511LV00017B/2610